W9-ARC-806

Understanding Genetics™

DNA and RNA

Linley Erin Hall

ROSEN PUBLISHING®

New York

Published in 2011 by The Rosen Publishing Group, Inc.
29 East 21st Street, New York, NY 10010

Copyright © 2011 by The Rosen Publishing Group, Inc.

First Edition

All rights reserved. No part of this book may be reproduced in any form without permission in writing from the publisher, except by a reviewer.

Library of Congress Cataloging-in-Publication Data

Hall, Linley Erin.
DNA and RNA / Linley Erin Hall. — 1st ed.
     p. cm. — (Understanding genetics)
Includes bibliographical references and index.
ISBN 978-1-4358-9532-4 (library binding)
1. DNA — Juvenile literature. 2. RNA — Juvenile literature. I. Title.
QP624.H35 2011
611'.018166 — dc22

                                                                2009046612

Manufactured in the United States of America

CPSIA Compliance Information: Batch #S10YA: For Further Information Contact Rosen Publishing, New York, New York
at 1-800-237-9932

On the cover: DNA and RNA are complex molecules that are key to life. DNA stores genetic information, whereas RNA allows that genetic information to be used by the cell.

611 HAL 756 25 E9 Trine acct 2011-2012 R Davis e. 3/20/12 #18⁰⁰

MAYO H.S. FOR MST LIBRARY

Contents

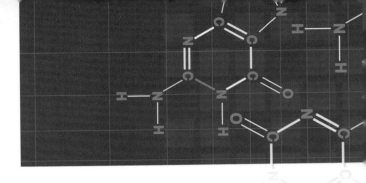

Introduction

A student goes to the library in search of a particular piece of information for an essay she is writing. She finds that the information is contained in a particular chapter of a book. This book is extremely important, and the librarians are afraid of it being damaged. Thus, the library keeps the book in a special room, and no one can take it out of this room. However, the room contains a photocopier. So the student makes a photocopy of the chapter of the book that she needs. Then she takes the copy into the main part of the library.

The book is also written in Chinese. The student must translate the chapter to English. Using the photocopy, she sits in the main part of the library and figures out what each of the Chinese characters means. Once she has finished the translation, she can finally write her essay using the information in the chapter.

This analogy describes how deoxyribonucleic acid, or DNA, and ribonucleic acid, or RNA, work together to make proteins. The DNA is the book containing the information. It's kept in a special compartment in the cell called the nucleus, which it cannot leave. However, copies of parts of the DNA can be made in the form of RNA. RNA is not an exact copy of the DNA, but it contains the information in the DNA, and RNA (the photocopy) can leave the nucleus.

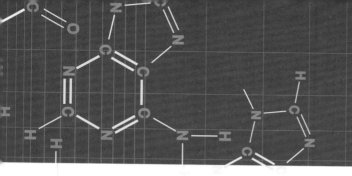

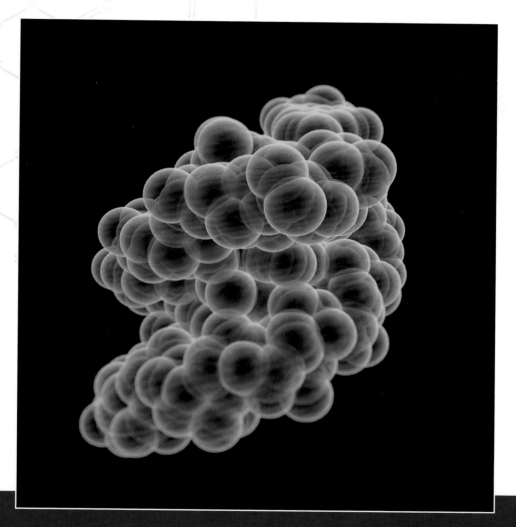

Under a high level of magnification, DNA looks like this. Each atom is represented by a sphere. The molecule contains all the instructions needed for an organism to function.

In the main part of the cell, the RNA is used to create proteins. This process is like translating the chapter from Chinese to English. The components of the RNA molecule are known as nucleotides. They must be translated into amino acids, which are the components of proteins. The proteins carry out the work of the cell. Without functional proteins, a cell can't do its job, and it may die. Thus, it's very important that the information contained in the DNA is translated faithfully.

The structure of DNA was discovered in 1953. Before then, there was evidence that it was the genetic material. But no one knew how the molecule could carry information. The discovery of the structure made that obvious. Over the last fifty or so years, huge gains have been made in our knowledge about how both DNA and RNA function. These molecules have allowed us to better understand inherited diseases and cancer, and create new tests and treatments for them. Discoveries about DNA and RNA have also allowed us to modify organisms by inserting DNA from another organism. In some cases, we have also changed human DNA.

The new technologies that use DNA and RNA have a lot of potential to help people. But they could cause problems. We need to be careful as we go into the future. A good understanding of the basics of DNA and RNA is an excellent place to begin.

CHAPTER one

Introduction to DNA

"DNA" is an abbreviation for deoxyribonucleic acid. DNA contains the instructions for making proteins. Proteins, in turn, do the work of the cell. Every living thing contains deoxyribonucleic acid, from the smallest of microorganisms to the largest of whales.

There are two types of cells: eukaryotic and prokaryotic. Prokaryotic cells are only found in bacteria and archaea. In fact, bacteria and archaea are prokaryotic cells, since they are single-celled organisms. Prokaryotic cells are very simple. The DNA in prokaryotic cells is mixed in with all the other molecules in the cell.

Eukaryotic cells are much larger and more complicated than prokaryotic cells. Eukaryotic cells contain a structure called the nucleus. The nucleus is where the cell keeps most of its DNA. The nuclear membrane helps protect the DNA from damage. A small amount of DNA is also located in structures called mitochondria and chloroplasts.

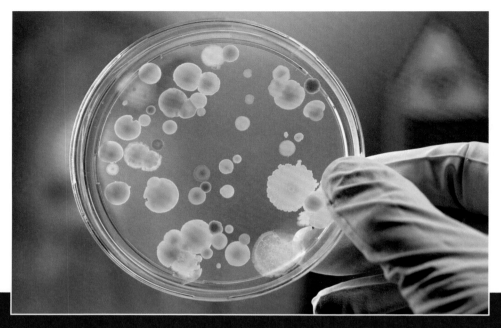

The bacteria growing on this agar plate are composed of prokaryotic cells. In these cells, DNA is not separated into its own compartment as in eukaryotic cells.

Components of DNA

Nucleic acids are composed of units called nucleotides. A DNA molecule may contain thousands or even millions of nucleotides. Each nucleotide is made from three smaller parts. These are a phosphate group, a sugar, and a nitrogen-containing base. The phosphate group is a phosphorus atom that is bonded to four oxygen atoms. The sugar in DNA is called deoxyribose. It's made of a ring of four carbon atoms and one oxygen atom.

The nitrogenous bases are molecules that contain rings of carbon and nitrogen atoms. DNA contains four different bases: adenine, thymine, cytosine, and guanine. These are often abbreviated as A, T, C, and G. Adenine and guanine both have structures

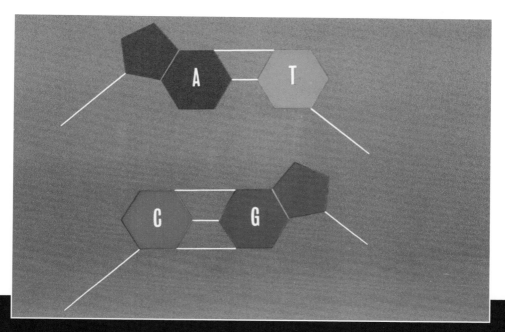

The nitrogeneous bases in DNA are adenosine (A), thymine (T), cytosine (C), and guanine (G). A and T always pair together, and C and G always pair together.

that contain two rings. Thymine and cytosine, on the other hand, only contain one ring each.

DNA Structure

So how do these components come together? Deoxyribose and the phosphate link together in alternation in a long chain to make up the backbone of the DNA molecule. The bases are attached to the sugars and seem to hang off the backbone. A single strand of DNA looks a bit like a comb with the bases as the teeth. The ends of the DNA strand are different. The 3' end (pronounced "three prime end") finishes with a sugar on the backbone, while the 5' end finishes with a phosphate.

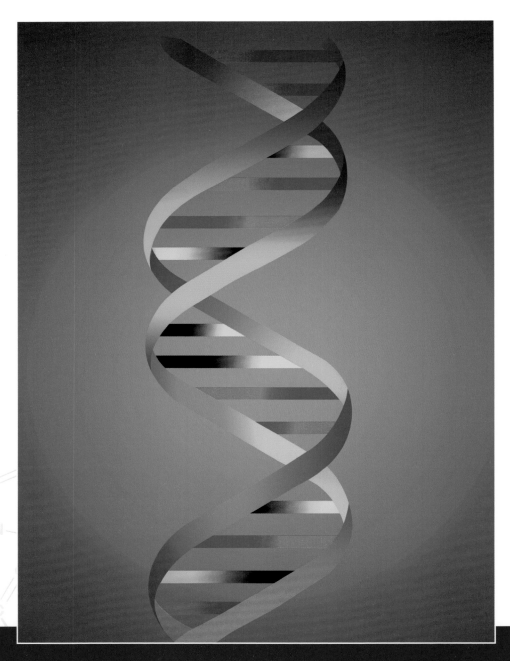

DNA is usually found in the form of a double helix. Two DNA strands are bound together, and the pair twists into a spiral.

But DNA is not usually single-stranded. Instead, two strands are bound to each other. The backbones run in opposite directions to each other, one being 3' to 5' while the other is 5' to 3'. The bases hanging off the backbone bind to each other to form a double helix. Adenine on one strand always binds to thymine on the other, and cytosine on one to guanine on the other. This means that a base with one ring always binds to a base with two rings. Thus, the A-T and C-G base pairs are about the same size.

An easy way to think about the double helix is as a ladder. The sugar-phosphate backbones are the sides of the ladder. The base pairs are the rungs. This ladder, however, is twisted, so that climbing the rungs of the ladder would feel like going up a spiral staircase.

Perhaps most important, the bases in a DNA molecule are not in random order. They are in a specific sequence. It's this sequence of A, T, C, and G that contains the instructions for making proteins.

Packaging DNA

Each human cell contains about three billion base pairs of DNA. Stretched out, this DNA would be several feet long. Cells are obviously much tinier than that, and nuclei are smaller still. To fit in the nucleus, DNA must fold up.

The DNA wraps around proteins called histones. These proteins allow DNA to become more compact. Wrapping around the histones also helps protect the DNA. Under a microscope, DNA wrapped around histones looks like beads on a string.

Around two hundred base pairs of DNA wrap around one set of histone proteins. There are five histone proteins, called H1, H2A, H2B, H3, and H4. H1 binds on its own to about fifty base pairs of DNA. Two copies of each of the other four histone proteins combine to create what is called the histone octamer. About 150 base pairs of DNA wrap twice around this octamer.

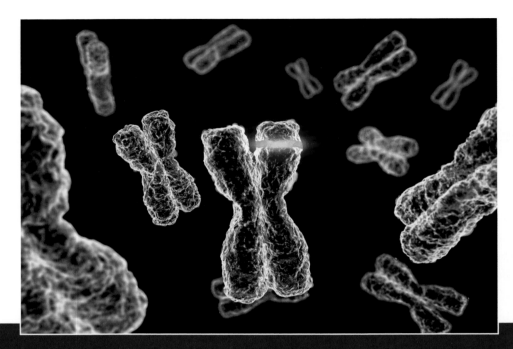

Cells do not contain one long DNA molecule. Instead, the organism's DNA is split into smaller strands, known as chromosomes, represented here by a computer-generated image.

In cells, DNA wrapped around histones rarely looks like beads on a string. Instead, the histones pack together to condense the DNA even further. This is a good way to store the DNA, but it must be unpacked and unwound for replication or other processes.

Chromosomes

In addition, the DNA in eukaryotic cells is not all in one long strand. It's divided into smaller strands called chromosomes. Each type of organism has its own unique number of chromosomes. Humans have forty-six. Butterflies have 380. The number of chromosomes has nothing to do with the complexity of an organism or how much DNA it has.

The Discovery of DNA Structure

In the early 1950s, many scientists were trying to figure out the structures of molecules important to living things. They had determined that DNA was the material of heredity. But without knowing its structure, scientists couldn't figure out how DNA carried information.

In early 1953, Linus Pauling published a paper on DNA's structure. He suggested that it was composed of three strands with their backbones bound together in the middle and their bases on the outside.

James Watson and Francis Crick, who had also been working on the problem, knew that Pauling's model had to be wrong. They proposed the double-stranded DNA structure that we now know to be correct. Watson and Crick determined the structure based on many pieces of information. One was X-ray patterns taken of DNA crystals by Rosalind Franklin. The pattern, known as Photo 51, showed that DNA had to be a helix. Watson and Crick also knew that experiments in Erwin Chargaff's laboratory had shown that the bases adenine and thymine occurred in equal amounts. So did cytosine and guanine. This suggested that these bases were paired somehow.

The two scientists built models of DNA in their laboratory. Using these visual aids helped Watson and Crick figure out how the helix was put together. Their DNA structure was quickly accepted as correct by other scientists. The two, along with Maurice Wilkins, received the Nobel Prize for their work in 1962. Sadly, by that time Franklin had died of cancer.

Chromosomes can be either linear or circular. Humans and other complex organisms have linear chromosomes. Many bacteria have circular chromosomes, however. Bacteria are prokaryotes, so their DNA isn't contained in a nucleus. Keeping the DNA in circles helps protect it.

A human's forty-six chromosomes are composed of twenty-three pairs. In each pair, one chromosome comes from the mother and one

Gregor Mendel discovered the basic rules of heredity in the 1860s. Sadly, his work was ignored for many years. Today, he is known as the Father of Modern Genetics.

from the father. One pair of chromosomes varies according to sex. Females have two X chromosomes, while males have one X and one Y chromosome. The twenty-two nonsex chromosomes are numbered roughly according to their length. Chromosome 1 is the longest, while chromosome 21 is the smallest (22 is slightly longer than 21).

Functions of DNA

Some parts of DNA are known as genes. Genes, units of heredity, contain the instructions to make proteins. Most eukaryotic organisms carry two copies of each gene, one on each pair of chromosomes. One gene is inherited from the mother and one from the father. Different forms (alleles) of the same gene can make an organism have different characteristics. Between 1856 and 1863, a monk named Gregor Mendel worked out the basic rules of heredity. In his experiments, he used pea plants. He found that some pea seeds were smooth while others were wrinkled, some yellow while others were green, and so on. He thought that each plant contained factors inherited from the parents that determined these characteristics. Later, when scientists studied DNA, they realized that the factors that Mendel described were actually genes in the DNA sequence.

Most human DNA is not genes, however. Some of this noncoding DNA helps signal where the genes are located and when they should be translated into proteins. The functions of other sections of DNA are mostly unknown. Nongene DNA is sometimes called junk DNA. Researchers first thought that the DNA outside of genes was worthless. Now they are realizing just how important some of this DNA is.

Every cell in an organism should contain exactly the same DNA. Making exact copies is not easy, but cells use many tools to make sure that it happens—most of the time. The next chapter looks at replication, the process in which strands of DNA are copied.

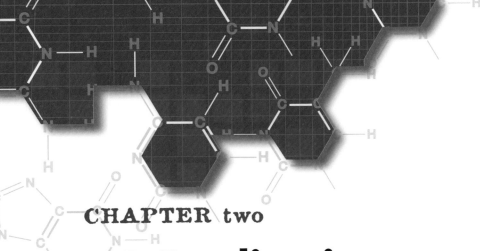

CHAPTER two

DNA Replication

Among the many things they do, cells also divide to create new cells. This cell division is important for growth, such as when teenagers get taller. Cells also eventually get old and die. Cell division helps make sure that young cells are available to take the place of the old ones. For example, people scrub off old, dead skin cells every time they shower. But they don't run out of skin because new skin cells are created constantly.

When it divides, a cell makes a copy of its DNA. This process is called replication. DNA replication is described as semiconservative. Each new DNA double helix contains one old DNA strand and one new one. The old one serves as a template for creating the new strand.

This chapter will explore the process of replication and its importance for organisms.

Mitosis and Meiosis

The nuclear division that happens in most cells of the body is called mitosis. Mitosis creates two new nuclei that are identical to the

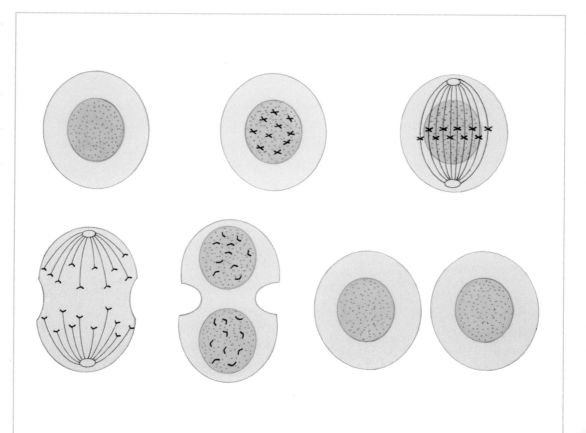

In mitosis, all of the cell's DNA is replicated. Then the chromosomes line up in the middle of the cell, and the two copies of each chromosome are pulled in opposite directions. Finally, a new cell membrane forms.

original nucleus. This requires that the cell replicate all the DNA in its nucleus. Each new cell needs its own complete set of instructions. After replication of the DNA, the nuclear membrane breaks up. The two sets of chromosomes are pulled to opposite ends of the cell. New nuclear membranes then form, and the cell itself divides, creating two new cells.

A few cells in the body divide using a different nuclear division process, which is called meiosis. Meiosis only happens in the sex organs, and it creates sex cells. The sex cells are called eggs, or ova, in women, and sperm in men. To create a new organism, one sperm combines with one egg. This combined cell, the zygote, needs to have the normal number of chromosomes for that particular species—forty-six in humans. Thus, each sex cell needs to have half that number—twenty-three in humans.

Meiosis is similar to mitosis at the start. All the DNA in the nucleus is replicated. Then, however, the pairs of chromosomes line up. They look like two letter X's beside each other because each old chromosome and its new copy are still connected. Now the chromosomes have an opportunity to swap DNA. For example, a portion of each chromosome 19 might break off and reattach to the other chromosome 19. This helps increase genetic diversity. The pairs of chromosomes are then pulled apart into two nuclei, cutting the number of chromosomes in each daughter nucleus in half. Each of these two new nuclei goes through another round of division. Meiosis and division of the cells yield four sex cells that contain half the usual number of chromosomes.

Replication

During cell division, enzymes enter the nucleus to signal to the DNA that it's time to replicate. Enzymes are proteins that catalyze reactions. They bring together molecules and help them interact. These particular enzymes help the DNA unwind from the histones. This makes the DNA more accessible for replication.

Then proteins called initiators scan the DNA strands. They search for sequences called origins. Origins are the places where DNA replication must start. An organism's DNA may contain up to one hundred thousand origins. Thus, replication occurs at many places at the same time. This speeds up the process.

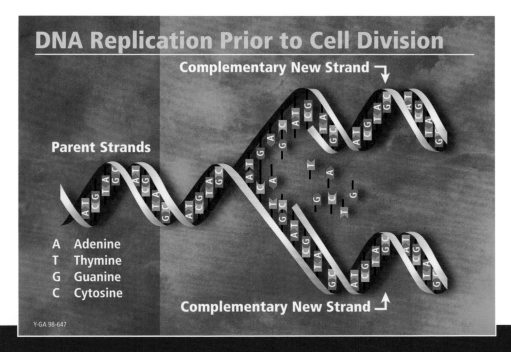

DNA Replication Prior to Cell Division

Complementary New Strand

Parent Strands

A   Adenine
T   Thymine
G   Guanine
C   Cytosine

Y-GA 98-647

Complementary New Strand

During DNA replication, the cell makes a new copy of each DNA strand using an existing strand as a template. This is known as semiconservative replication and helps prevent mistakes.

Once an initiator finds an origin, it breaks apart the two DNA strands, separating the complementary bases. Then an enzyme, called helicase, opens the DNA even farther. It may separate hundreds of base pairs. Single-stranded binding proteins attach to the DNA to help it stay open. Another protein, called gyrase, helps prevent the DNA from becoming twisted.

At each end of the bubble of open DNA there is a replication fork where the DNA goes from being single-stranded to double-stranded. Let's focus on what happens at just one of these forks. One strand runs toward the fork in the 5' to 3' direction. It's known as the leading strand. The other strand is the lagging strand.

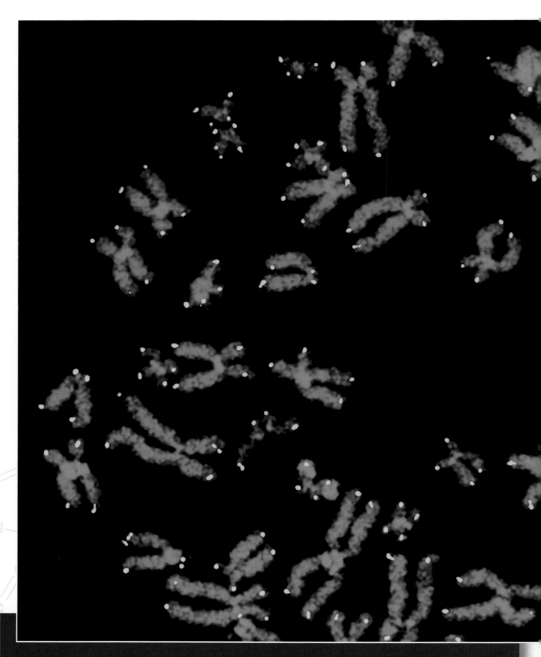

Telomeres, the DNA at the ends of chromosomes, are colored yellow here. They help protect genes from damage. When telomeres grow too short, the cell dies.

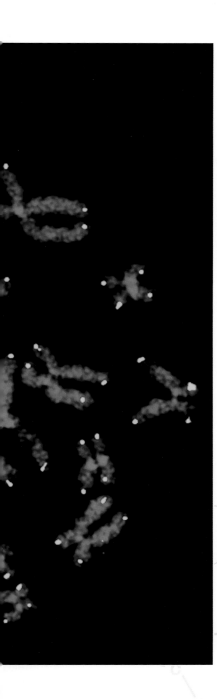

One or more nucleotides of temporary RNA bond to the bases first opened in the origin. These are known as primers, and they help get things moving. A protein called DNA polymerase then begins to move down the leading strand. As it goes, it determines the next base in line and attaches the complementary nucleotide. Lots of these nucleotides are floating in the nucleus, ready to become part of the DNA strand.

Unfortunately, DNA polymerase only works in the 5' to 3' direction. As more bases open up at the replication fork, the DNA of the lagging strand is replicated in the 5' to 3' direction in short bursts known as Okazaki fragments. Each fragment gets its own RNA primers.

Eventually, the DNA polymerase on the leading strand reaches the next origin, where replication has already occurred. Enzymes then remove the RNA primers and the appropriate DNA nucleotides are inserted. The protein ligase then links all the new DNA strands.

Tying Up Loose Ends

The process of replication is generally fast and accurate. However, mistakes can happen. Occasionally, DNA

The Human Genome Project and Gene Sequencing

The Human Genome Project was an international collaboration between scientists working to find the sequence of bases in human DNA. The genome is just an organism's entire complement of DNA. In humans, these are chromosomes 1 through 22, plus the X and Y chromosomes. The rough draft of the human genome was released in the year 2001 and the final draft in 2003. Since then, researchers have used the information in many experiments.

DNA replication was a key part of the Human Genome Project. It allowed the researchers to determine the sequence of the DNA. The sequencing method is known as the chain termination or Sanger method, after Frederick Sanger, its inventor.

Dideoxynucleotides are similar to regular DNA nucleotides, except they lack one of the chemical groups that help the normal deoxynucleotides link to one another. Once a dideoxynucleotide is incorporated into a DNA strand, replication stops because there is nothing for the next nucleotide to attach to. Dideoxynucleotides can be labeled with fluorescent dyes that make them glow different colors.

To sequence a DNA sample of interest, scientists combine lots of copies of the DNA of interest, the RNA and proteins necessary for replication, regular DNA nucleotides, and small amounts of the fluorescent dideoxynucleotides. As replication progresses, usually regular nucleotides will be incorporated. But sometimes a dideoxynucleotide will be added to the growing strand. Replication will thus stop at this point. This creates DNA strands of many different lengths.

After replication finishes, scientists use a technique called gel electrophoresis to separate the strands according to their size. Each size of strand shows up as a band at a different place in the gel. Each band glows a different color depending on the dideoxynucleotide it contains. Using these colors, researchers can read the DNA sequence along the gel.

During the Human Genome Project, researchers harnessed DNA replication to sequence all DNA in a human being. This information is being used to learn more about the human body and fight disease.

Improvements in technology continue to make genome sequencing faster and cheaper. Recently, the genome of James Watson, codiscoverer of the DNA structure, was sequenced in a few months for around $2 million. Eventually, genome sequencing will likely be inexpensive enough for everyone to do it.

polymerase mismatches bases. It might pair a thymine with a guanine, for example. An enzyme called proofreading DNA polymerase looks for mismatched bases in the new DNA strand. When it finds errors, it removes the wrong nucleotide and inserts the correct one.

The cell also needs to clean up the ends of the chromosomes. These are known as telomeres. The DNA in telomeres does not code for proteins. Instead, telomeres protect the important information in the DNA molecule. After replication, the DNA has single-stranded ends. In meiosis, an enzyme called telomerase adds more bases to the end of the DNA so that it is entirely double-stranded. In contrast, in mitosis these single-stranded ends are just chopped off. Thus, the telomeres get shorter every time the cell divides. When the telomeres get too short, the cell dies. This is part of normal aging.

Although DNA is crucial, it couldn't direct the activities of the cell without its sidekick, RNA. The next chapter looks at the differences between DNA and RNA.

CHAPTER three

Introduction to RNA

RNA is an abbreviation for ribonucleic acid. It's similar to DNA in many ways. RNA and DNA contain many of the same components, for example. But RNA is a more versatile molecule than DNA. It can do things that DNA can only dream of.

RNA is made in the nucleus of the cell. DNA is used as the template for manufacturing RNA. The process is known as transcription, and chapter 4 will explain it in more depth. After being made in the nucleus, RNA moves into the cytoplasm to do its work.

Components of RNA

Like DNA, RNA nucleotides contain a phosphate, a sugar, and a base. The phosphate is exactly the same. The sugar, however, is a bit different. The sugar in RNA is ribose. It contains one more oxygen atom than deoxyribose, the sugar in DNA. (Indeed, the "deoxy" in deoxyribose indicates that it is ribose that is missing an oxygen atom.)

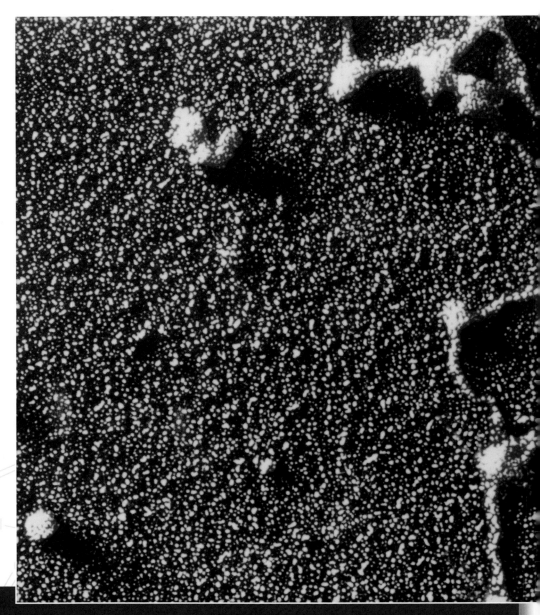

This electron micrograph shows RNA polymerase molecules attached to strands of DNA. RNA polymerase is one of the many proteins involved in creating strands of RNA using DNA as a template.

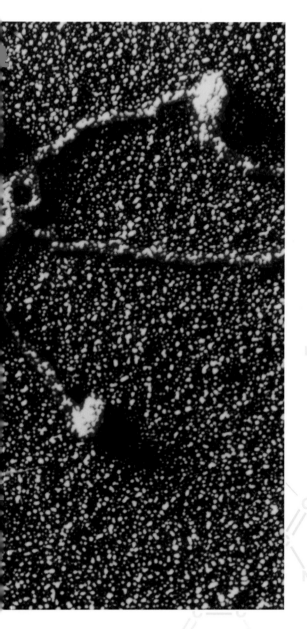

RNA also contains four nitrogenous bases. Three of these are the same as in DNA: guanine, cytosine, and adenine. However, RNA contains the base uracil instead of thymine. The structures of uracil and thymine are similar, and uracil prefers to bond with adenine. However, uracil can bond to cytosine and guanine. This is an important characteristic.

DNA vs. RNA

RNA thus has two changes that make it more reactive: ribose instead of deoxyribose, and uracil instead of thymine. Why is it important for RNA to be more reactive than DNA? DNA's function is to keep the genetic material safe. Thus, being less likely to react with other molecules is important. On the other hand, RNA needs to react with other molecules as it fulfills its function of making proteins.

Another big difference between RNA and DNA has to do with their structures. DNA is a double-stranded molecule. RNA is

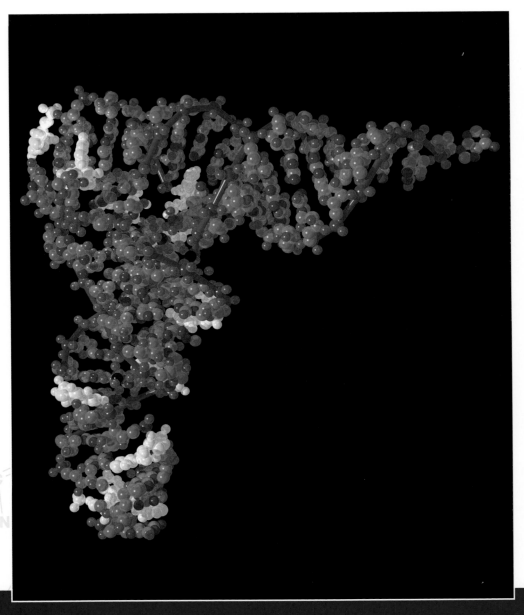

This molecular model depicts the transfer RNA for the amino acid phenylalanine. Common atoms in RNA include oxygen (red), carbon (green), and nitrogen (blue). RNA also includes hydrogen and phosphorus.

almost always a single-stranded molecule. This makes it more unstable than DNA. After RNA has fulfilled its function, it falls apart. The nucleotides are then used to make other RNA molecules.

However, RNA's single strand can fold into a lot of different shapes, many more than DNA. This is where the ability of uracil to bond with any of the other bases comes in handy. Uracil's bonding helps RNA stay in different shapes. These shapes depend on what the particular RNA molecule's function is. In addition, some RNA molecules contain sequences that are complementary. The RNA can thus fold over and form a double-stranded molecule with itself. This helps increase the stability of the RNA when that is important for its function.

Types of RNA

There are many different types of RNA. The three most common types are known as messenger RNA (mRNA), transfer RNA (tRNA), and ribosomal RNA (rRNA). All types of RNA are created using DNA as a template. This is known as transcription. However, after transcription the various RNAs fold into different shapes and fulfill very distinct functions.

Messenger RNA is a transcript of a gene. This means that each mRNA molecule carries the instructions for making a protein. After it is made in the nucleus through a process called transcription, mRNA travels into the cytoplasm to a ribosome.

Ribosomes are the protein-making factories in the cell. They are composed of about 65 percent ribosomal RNA and 35 percent protein. Some ribosomes are attached to the endoplasmic reticulum, another structure in the cell. Others float around in the cytoplasm. Ribosomes have two subunits, a small one and a large one. The mRNA slides through the small subunit, which reads it. The large subunit builds the corresponding protein.

RNA and the Origin of Life

Some scientists used to wonder why RNA is necessary. Why not just make proteins directly from DNA?

Several decades ago, Francis Crick, one of the discoverers of the structure of DNA, suggested that RNA came before DNA. That is, when life was just beginning on Earth, organisms used RNA to encode their genetic material instead of DNA. Crick thought that this early RNA was able to catalyze its own replication. In Crick's theory, DNA was a later development in the evolution of life. Its more stable structure helped organisms protect their genetic material.

In the early 1980s, two scientists, Thomas Cech and Sidney Altman, showed that some RNA can catalyze reactions. Then, in the 1990s, Harry Noller showed that the RNA in the ribosome actually links amino acids together into a protein. Previously, scientists had thought that the proteins in the ribosome did this.

These discoveries added support to the idea that an "RNA world" existed before the "DNA world" we know today. Today, most scientists believe that RNA came before DNA, though we may never know for sure.

Francis Crick (third from left) *suggested that RNA might have come before DNA in the evolution of life. Today, most scientists believe that this was the case.*

Transfer RNA transports amino acids to the ribosome. Amino acids are the building blocks of proteins. tRNA molecules are adapters, a bit like a power adapter for a laptop computer. On one end of the tRNA is a site where an amino acid can attach. A family of enzymes called aminoacyl tRNA synthetases attaches the amino acids to the appropriate tRNA molecules.

On the other end of the tRNA is a sequence of three bases. This is known as an anticodon. It is complementary to a sequence of three bases in the messenger RNA. This mRNA sequence is known as a codon. The amino acid attachment site is specific to the amino acid that corresponds to the codon that matches the tRNA's anticodon.

For example, the codon for the amino acid methionine is AUG. The anticodon on the tRNA that carries methionine is UAC. The ribosome matches the

RNA Viruses

DNA is the genetic material for almost all organisms. However, some viruses use RNA as their genetic material. Viruses are not cells. They are basically a shell made out of protein around some nucleic acid, either DNA or RNA. Viruses are parasites. They hijack cells in order to reproduce themselves. Many viruses cause disease. The human immunodeficiency virus (HIV), which causes AIDS, is an RNA virus.

In organisms, DNA serves as the template to make RNA. But RNA-based viruses contain a protein called reverse transcriptase. Once a virus enters a cell, this enzyme can make single-stranded DNA using RNA as a template. Then the virus makes double-stranded DNA from the single strand. Finally, the virus inserts its DNA into the host cell's genome. The cell then starts making viral proteins from this DNA.

codons and anticodons when it puts together a new protein. The next chapter will explain this process, which is called translation.

RNA molecules are also involved in regulating genes. In eukaryotes, small RNAs known as microRNAs can prevent messenger RNA from being translated or make mRNA degrade faster. This process is called RNA interference. In prokaryotes, CRISPR RNAs perform a similar function. Some cells contain antisense RNA, which is complementary to strands of mRNA. The antisense RNA binds to the mRNA, which prevents it from being translated. This is one way that cells control how much of certain proteins is made. In addition, small nuclear RNA is found in spliceosomes. These complexes of protein and snRNA help process other types of RNA after they are transcribed. Scientists are still learning about all the different types of RNA and the functions they can perform.

CHAPTER four

Transcription and Translation

RNA is a go-between for DNA and proteins. Transcription is the process in which RNA molecules are made from DNA. Translation is the process in which this RNA is used to create proteins. Both of these processes are essential to the life of the cell.

Transcription

In transcription, DNA serves as a template to make RNA. RNA contains some different components than DNA, so transcription does not create an exact copy the way replication does. But the RNA created in transcription contains the information in the DNA sequence—the base sequence in the RNA corresponds to the base sequence in the DNA. This is the most important part.

mRNA, tRNA, and rRNA molecules are all formed by the same transcription mechanism. At the beginning of transcription, a group of proteins called a holoenzyme complex scans the DNA. It looks for the promoter sequence of the gene to be transcribed. The

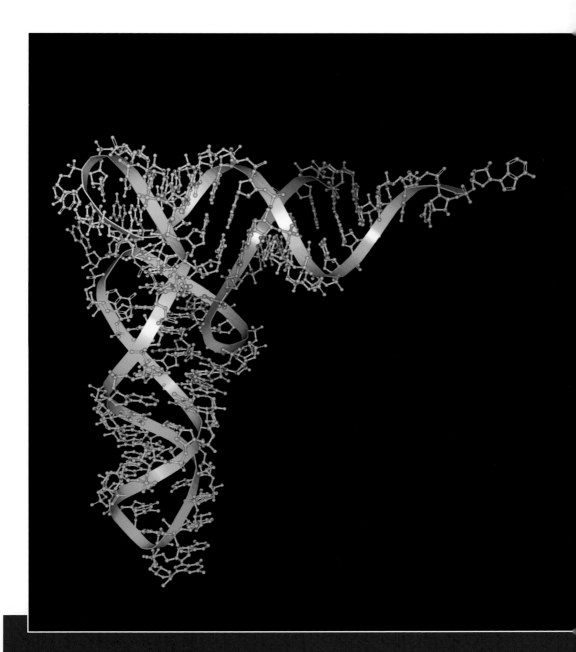

At the bottom of this tRNA molecule is the anticodon arm, which contains the anticodon that matches up with the mRNA codon during protein synthesis.

promoter is often a TATA box, so called because it contains a repeating T-A-T-A sequence.

The holoenzyme complex binds to the promoter and makes a small break in the DNA. This allows an enzyme called RNA polymerase to access the base pairs. RNA polymerase breaks apart about twenty base pairs, creating a bubble in the DNA. Then it uses RNA nucleotides that are floating in the nucleus to create a strand of RNA that is complementary to the DNA. This process is called elongation because the RNA strand becomes longer.

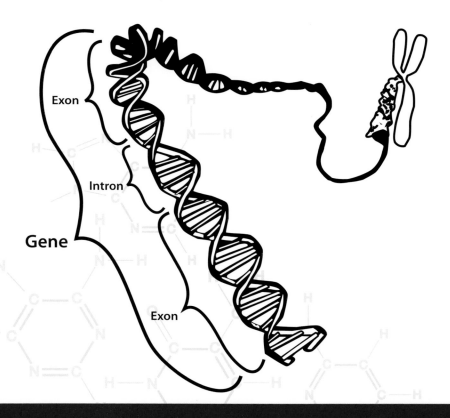

Genes in eukaryotic cells contain introns and exons. The introns are intervening sequences that must be edited out of the mRNA transcript before translation. Exons contain the instructions for making proteins.

As the RNA strand grows, it is pushed away from the DNA, and the bubble closes. Only a bubble of about twenty base pairs is open at one time. This helps protect the DNA.

Eventually, the RNA polymerase reaches a terminator sequence in the DNA. This sequence signals that the end of the gene has been reached. The RNA detaches from the DNA, and the DNA closes fully.

RNA Processing Post-Transcription

However, the RNA strand is not yet ready. Almost every eukaryotic gene contains sequences called introns and exons. The exons are the parts that code for protein and are most important. The introns are intervening sequences that do not code for protein. These must be removed.

Researchers are not sure what the purpose of introns is. Some have dismissed them as junk DNA that is completely useless. Others think that at least some introns may be important in regulating processes involving DNA. More research is needed to understand these sequences.

A complex of RNA and protein subunits called a spliceosome snips out the introns and binds the exons together. Researchers used to think that one gene always yields one protein. However, we now know that isn't true. The spliceosome can edit the RNA in different ways. By leaving out one or more exons, it can create different proteins. Human genes are particularly good at this. This different editing is one reason why we don't have as many genes as one would expect for such a complex organism. Many human genes can produce multiple proteins, so fewer genes are needed.

After intron removal, the RNA also receives a guanine cap on its leading end and adenines on its tail. These help prevent the RNA from falling apart too quickly. The RNA is now ready to leave the nucleus and get to work.

Translation

Translation uses the information in the mRNA to create a protein. Most organisms, including humans, use a set of twenty different amino acids to make proteins. Scientists found that a sequence of three bases on an mRNA molecule corresponds to one amino acid. These triplets of bases are codons.

There are sixty-four different codons. Some amino acids are coded for by more than one codon, but no codons respond to more than one amino acid. One codon, AUG, is the start signal. It also codes for the amino acid methionine. Thus, all proteins start with methionine at first, though it is sometimes removed later. In addition, three codons do not code for any amino acids at all. These codons—UAG, UAA, and UGA—are the stop signals.

At the beginning of translation, mRNA forms a complex with the small subunit of a ribosome. The mRNA slides along the subunit until the start codon, AUG, reaches the active site. Next, a tRNA molecule carrying a methionine joins the complex.

After the tRNA carrying methionine binds its anticodon to the mRNA start codon, the large subunit of the ribosome links up to the small subunit. The large subunit of the ribosome contains three slots called A, P, and E. tRNA molecules fit in the A and P slots such that their anticodons line up with the codons of the mRNA. When the subunits link up, the methionine tRNA starts out in the P slot of the large subunit.

Let's say that the second codon on the mRNA is GGG, which codes for glycine. A glycine-carrying tRNA with the anticodon CCC would enter the A slot of the ribosome. Ribosomal RNA then bonds

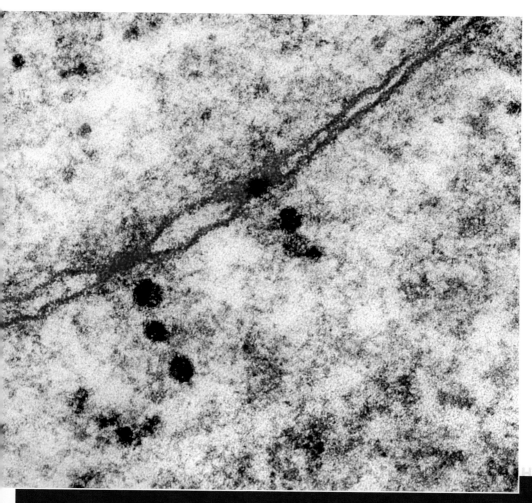

In this transmission electron micrograph, the ribosomes are colored blue. These structures are composed of rRNA and proteins and are the sites of protein synthesis, which also requires tRNA and mRNA.

the two amino acids together. In this process, the methionine is detached from its tRNA in the first slot. That tRNA moves to the E slot and then leaves the ribosome to pick up another methionine from the cytoplasm. The mRNA slides over, and the glycine tRNA slides

Cracking the Codon

In the late 1950s, researchers knew that DNA makes RNA, which makes protein. They also knew what the structure of DNA was. But it wasn't clear how nucleic acids were translated into amino acids.

With only four bases in RNA (C, G, A, and U) and twenty amino acids, each base couldn't code for one amino acid. Neither could pairs of amino acids be right because there were only sixteen possibilities. But triplets gave sixty-four possibilities, many more than necessary.

Francis Crick and Sydney Brenner did the experiments that established that the code is made of triplets. They found that if they deleted one, two, or four base pairs from a gene, they ended up with nonfunctional proteins. If they deleted three bases, however, one amino acid would be missing, but the rest of the protein would be OK.

Then Marshall Nirenberg and Heinrich Matthaei created an mRNA strand that was completely made of uracil. This yielded a protein that was made entirely of the amino acid phenylalanine. Thus, the triplet UUU had to translate to phenylalanine. A variety of other experiments were conducted to determine the other triplets.

As expected, many triplets coded for the same amino acid. Often, these codons differ just in their last letter. For example, the codons GCT, GCA, GCG, and GCC all code for the amino acid alanine. Researchers now think that the first and second letters in a triplet are examined most closely during protein synthesis. In additions, investigations showed that only sixty-one codons correspond to amino acids. The others signal for translation to stop. It took several years, but scientists eventually cracked the code.

This is a reconstruction of the model used by Watson and Crick to discover the double-helix structure of DNA. It is constructed out of metal plates and rods, some of which are the original ones the researchers used.

MATC INST FOR MST LIBRARY

with it, moving from the A slot to the P slot. Then, another tRNA can slide into the A slot.

This process repeats over and over to elongate the amino acid chain. This chain hangs off one of the tRNA molecules in the ribosome. It is passed from tRNA to tRNA as the chain gets longer.

Eventually, the ribosome reaches a stop codon. No tRNAs have anticodons that correspond to stop codons. Proteins called release factors recognize the stop signal and detach the protein product from the final tRNA. Other proteins help the new amino acid chain fold into a functional protein. Then the protein goes off to do its work. The last tRNA exits the ribosome so that all slots are empty.

The ribosome is then ready to create a new protein. The tRNA molecules are also reused over and over. The mRNA may be read multiple times depending on how much of a particular protein is needed. It usually disintegrates relatively quickly, however.

Transcription and translation are essential processes in a cell. But how does a cell know which genes to translate when? The next chapter looks at how cells control the expression of genes.

CHAPTER five

Gene Regulation

Humans have more than two hundred different types of cells. Sex cells contain only half of an organism's number of chromosomes. Red blood cells do not have nuclei and thus have no DNA. But all other human cell types contain a complete set of DNA, which is forty-six chromosomes. Thus, all cells contain the instructions for making every protein that an organism could want to make.

However, most cells don't need to make all those proteins. A muscle cell and a skin cell obviously have different functions. And they need different proteins to carry out these functions. As a result, different genes are active in skin cells and muscle cells. Genes that are unnecessary in a particular type of cell are turned off early in development. But even within a certain type of cell, different genes may be more or less active at different times.

Cells turn genes off and on at different times through gene regulation. Genes are regulated in response to a variety of factors. The processes that prokaryotes and eukaryotes use to regulate genes are different. The basic idea is the same, however: A protein should only be made when it is needed.

Gene Regulation in Prokaryotes

Bacteria and other prokaryotes are single-celled organisms. Thus, shutting off genes due to cell specialization isn't an issue. However, prokaryotes turn genes off and on depending on their environment. When a particular nutrient is available, bacteria may activate genes that code for proteins that digest that nutrient. When a nutrient is not available, bacteria may activate genes that code for proteins that build that nutrient out of other molecules. Prokaryotes may also activate or deactivate genes in response to heat, light, moisture, and other characteristics of the world around them. Turning genes on and off allows bacteria to respond to their environment and use their energy and nutrients efficiently.

Prokaryotes mainly regulate their genes using repressors. Repressors reduce the amount of mRNA that is created from a gene. These proteins bind to the DNA near the beginning of the gene. They often make it so that RNA polymerase cannot bind to the promoter. Thus, the gene is not transcribed.

An example of how repressors work is found in the bacterium *E. coli*. *E. coli* lives in human intestines and is a favorite experimental subject for scientists. *E. coli* digests sugars, just like humans do. Under normal conditions, it cannot digest lactose, a sugar found in dairy products. One of the proteins involved in lactose digestion, called beta-galactosidase, breaks the lactose into two smaller sugars. When no lactose is present, *E. coli* regulates the beta-galactosidase gene so that the protein isn't produced.

E. coli has a repressor that can block the transcription of the beta-galactosidase gene. When no lactose is present, this repressor binds to the DNA sequence near the beginning of the beta-galactosidase gene. When lactose is present and there is little of the normal food sugar glucose, the lactose itself binds to the repressor. The repressor can't bind to DNA when it has lactose bound to it. This allows

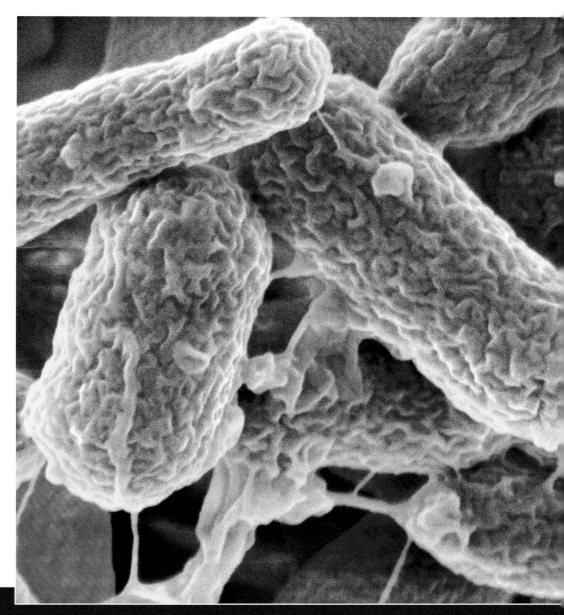

Bacteria are single-celled organisms. These E. coli *cells live in human intestines and help people digest food. Bacteria can turn genes off and on depending on the nutrients available.*

transcription of the beta-galactosidase gene to occur.

Gene Regulation in Eukaryotes: Transcription Factors

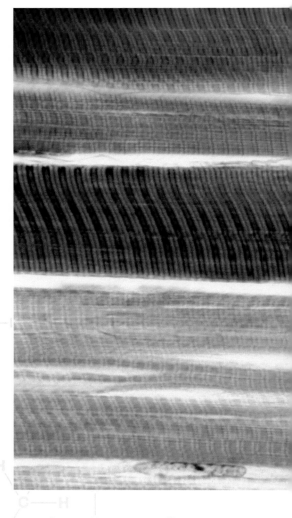

Eukaryotes regulate their genes in many different ways. The regulation can occur at many different points during transcription and translation.

Prokaryotes use repressors to turn genes off. Eukaryotes, on the other hand, use activators to turn genes on. These activators are known as transcription factors. Transcription factors are proteins. Not all cells contain all transcription factors. A muscle cell will contain a particular set, while a skin cell will contain a different set. The presence or absence of particular transcription factors differentiates cells.

Some transcription factors are present in all cells, but are not active all the time. For example, almost all organisms have a set of genes that are activated when it gets very hot. These are known as heat shock genes. The heat shock transcription factor controls them and is always present. However, it is only active when the temperature rises above a certain level.

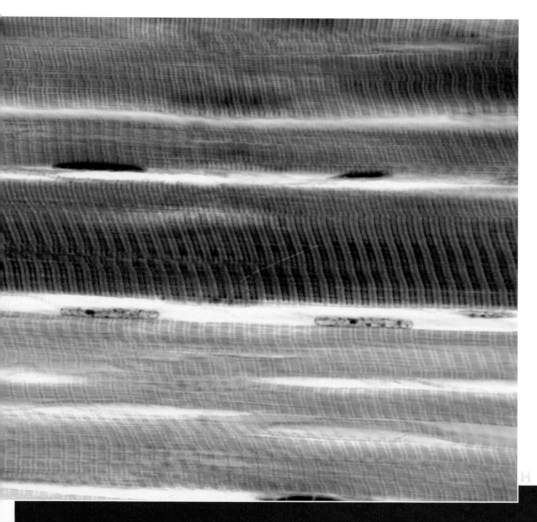

Skeletal muscle cells, like these pictured, need different proteins than skin cells. Thus, different sets of genes are turned on in the two types of cells.

Signals from molecules outside the cell can also activate transcription factors and thus genes. Growth factors and hormones are two of these molecules. The flood of hormones that comes during puberty causes many different changes. Teens grow taller and grow more

Other Ways to Regulate Eukaryotic Genes

Preventing transcription seems like the most efficient way to regulate genes. However, eukaryotes can also regulate genes farther down the path toward a protein.

After an mRNA has been transcribed, it must be processed before it can be translated. One way that eukaryotes regulate genes is by not processing mRNAs. Eukaryotic cells can also regulate genes by not translating mRNAs. Without translation, no protein is made. This kind of regulation often occurs during development. For example, the egg cells of many animals contain a lot of mRNA. However, these mRNAs are not translated unless the egg is fertilized. Scientists are still figuring out how cells prevent translation from occurring until they're ready.

Many of the mRNAs in egg cells code for transcription factors. These mRNAs are grouped in different parts of the egg. When the egg is fertilized and starts dividing, these mRNAs end up in different cells. Depending on the transcription factors it contains, a cell will become muscle or skin or another type of cell. RNA and transcription factors are thus extremely important for proper development of an organism because they appear to determine which genes are turned on and off in many cases.

Eukaryotic cells also regulate their genes through RNA degradation. All mRNA molecules are degraded after a few minutes to an hour. How quickly an mRNA is degraded depends on the sequence of the 3' untranslated region, or UTR. All mRNA molecules have this region on their 3' end that does not code for protein. The sequence AUUUA in the 3' UTR signals that the mRNA should be degraded quickly. Sometimes this sequence appears many times in the 3' UTR. This signals very fast degradation. Other mRNA molecules do not contain this sequence at all. They are degraded much more slowly.

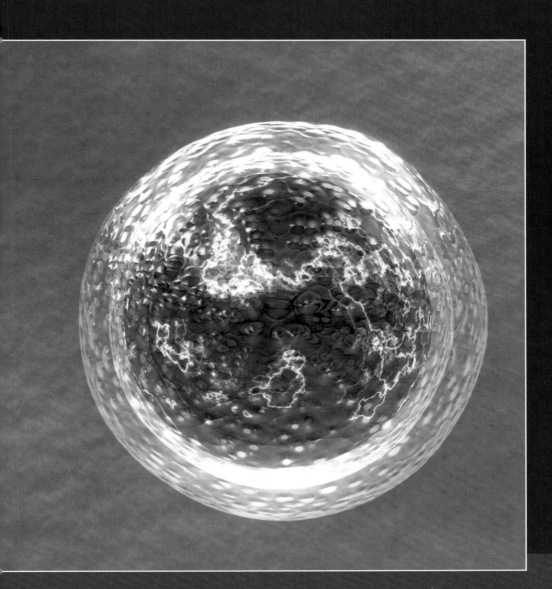

This egg cell contains a lot of mRNA. However, if the egg cell is not fertilized, many of those mRNAs will never be translated into proteins.

body hair. Girls develop breasts and begin to menstruate. Boys' voices deepen. All these changes occur because the hormones are activating transcription factors.

Hormones must bind to specific receptors on or in the cell to have an effect. Some hormones cannot cross the cell membrane. They bind to receptors located on the surface of the cell. This sets off a set of chemical reactions that causes the activation of a transcription factor. Other hormones can enter the cell. They bind to transcription factors directly. Without a hormone bound to them, these transcription factors are inactive. With a hormone bound, however, they are active and will cause transcription to occur. Some other hormones inactivate transcription factors by binding to them.

Cells have many different ways of determining how much of which proteins are made. These methods focus on preventing the transcription or translation of the DNA or RNA. But what happens when something is wrong with the DNA? The next chapter will look at the consequences of changes to the DNA sequence.

CHAPTER six

Mutations for Good and Bad

$\mathbf{T}$he word "mutation" often makes people think of horribly deformed creatures, such as three-eyed fish. Other people may think of comic book superheroes who gained their powers through mutations. But most real-life mutations are not nearly so dramatic.

A mutation is simply a change in the DNA sequence of an organism. The DNA replication process is very good, but not perfect. Sometimes mistakes are made. These mistakes are mutations. Mutations can also result from exposure to radiation, certain chemicals, or particular viruses. By wearing sunscreen out in the sun or a lead vest during dental X-rays, people protect themselves from mutations.

Some mutations are beneficial to an organism. For example, an inherited mutation could cause a moth to be darker colored than other moths. This dark color helps the moth hide from predators. Because the moth is not eaten, it has more children than other moths. Some of these baby moths would also have the beneficial mutation, escape predators, and have lots of kids themselves. Over time, the moth population could come to mostly or entirely be made of individuals

The ultraviolet radiation emitted by the sun can cause mutations in DNA. These mutations can lead to skin cancer. Wearing sunscreen helps protect the body from these mutations.

that had the mutation for dark color. This is natural selection at work. Organisms that contain beneficial characteristics are more likely to reproduce, so over time these characteristics can become standard in the population.

Other mutations have no effect at all on an organism. Without looking at the DNA code, no one will know that they are there. Still other mutations are very bad. They can cause disease and even death. Fortunately, new technologies are allowing us to test for these mutations and treat some diseases earlier.

DNA Sequence Mutations

Several different kinds of mutations can occur in a DNA sequence. The first is a point mutation. This is a substitution of one base for another, an A instead of a T, for example. A point mutation can have three consequences. First, it may do nothing at all. The bases in DNA are transcribed into mRNA. And, in most cases, multiple codons in the mRNA correspond to the same amino acid. For example, UGC and UGU both code for cysteine. Thus, a mutation

A DNA researcher compares the electrophoresis gels of two DNA sequences. Differences in the sequences are mutations. Mutations occur for many different reasons, but often do not cause harm to the organism.

that changes a UGU codon to UGC won't have any effect because the same amino acid ends up in the protein. This is known as a silent mutation.

However, changing a UGU codon to UGG means that tryptophan will be incorporated into the protein instead of cysteine. This substitution of one amino acid for another is known as a missense mutation. The effect of a missense mutation depends on where the amino acid is located in the protein and what its role is.

Finally, changing a UGU codon to UGA is a big problem. UGA is one of the three stop codons. This mutation will terminate transcription of the mRNA early. This is known as a nonsense mutation. Nonsense mutations almost always result in nonfunctional proteins.

Of course, substitution of one base for another is not the only way mutations can occur. Sometimes a base pair is added or deleted. This is easier to understand using words instead of codons. Think about the sentence LET MAX THE DOG RUN. Say that the M is deleted. The sentence would then read LET AXT HED OGR UN. It doesn't make any sense. The reading frame has been changed. An addition or subtraction of two base pairs also changes the reading frame. But addition or subtraction of three base pairs simply adds or deletes an amino acid. In the sentence above, say that M, A, and X were deleted. LET THE DOG RUN is still an understandable sentence, just a shorter one. Sometimes adding or removing an amino acid will cause a big change in a protein. Other times it may have no effect.

Chromosome Mutations

Mutations can also occur when chromosomes swap DNA during meiosis. Pieces of DNA that are the same size are supposed to be exchanged. But sometimes chromosomes exchange pieces of different sizes. This means that one chromosome is now missing genes, while the other chromosome has two copies. Other times

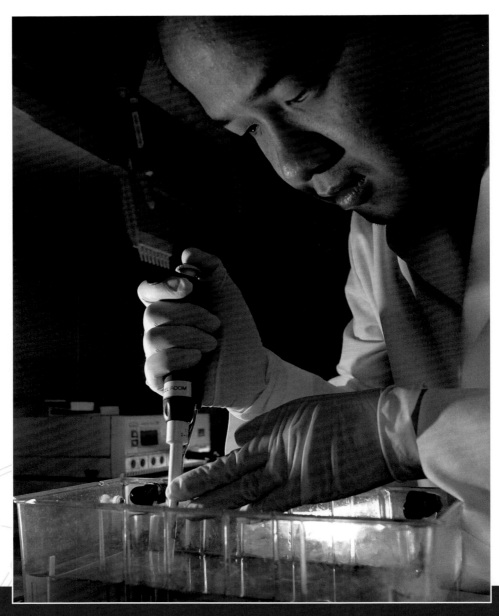

A scientist at the UCSF Comprehensive Cancer Center checks for variations in genetic samples that would point to a person's likelihood of developing lung, prostate, breast, or colorectal cancer.

chromosomes will swap DNA of the same size, but the DNA attaches to the chromosome upside down. Or, sometimes the chromosomes don't separate properly during meiosis, and one sex cell ends up with two copies of a particular chromosome while another contains zero.

All of these chromosomal mutations can cause abnormalities in an organism. In fact, mothers pregnant with fetuses with these kinds of mutations often miscarry because the fetus is unable to survive. However, some chromosomal mutations do not result in death. For example, Down syndrome occurs when someone has three copies of chromosome 21.

Mutations and Cancer

Mutations that occur in nonsex cells can lead to cancer. This is particularly true for mutations in genes that code for growth factors, which are proteins that control the speed of cell division. Mutations in growth factors can cause cells to grow out of control, which is a characteristic of cancer. These mutations are often caused by exposure to radiation or chemicals.

Some mutated genes that make a person more likely to get cancer are passed down in families. For example, mutations in the BRCA1 and BRCA2 genes are linked to breast cancer. Having mutations in these genes does not mean that someone will definitely get cancer, but it makes it more likely.

People can choose to be tested for mutations in the BRCA1 and BRCA2 genes, as well as others known to be associated with cancer or other diseases. People usually choose to be tested if they have a family history of a disease. If people do have a mutation, they may be able to take various steps to reduce their risk of developing the disease. They may also decide to use reproductive technologies to avoid passing the mutated gene down to their children.

Tracing History Through DNA

Some scientists have used mutations in DNA to trace the evolution and migration of humans in history.

In eukaryotes, the nucleus is not the only structure in the cell that contains DNA. Structures called mitochondria also have DNA. Mitochondria are passed from mothers to their children. If no mutations occur, a mother and her children will have exactly the same mitochondrial DNA.

In a 1987 article in the journal Nature, scientists looked at the mitochondrial DNA of people from different ethnic groups living in different parts of the world. They compared the sequences to find which mutations were shared by many groups and which ones by few groups. Mutations shared by many groups must have occurred earlier than mutations shared by just a few groups. They used this information to draw a "human family tree." This tree suggested that all living humans had a common ancestor that lived 140,000 to 290,000 years ago. Many people were shocked by this result. Scientists had believed that humans' common ancestor lived two million years ago.

In 2000, another group of scientists did a similar study using DNA from Y-chromosomes. Only men have Y-chromosomes. If no mutations occur, a father and son will have exactly the same Y-chromosome. The human family tree found in this study was similar to the mitochondrial tree. It suggested a common ancestor about 150,000 years ago. This research has made scientists reconsider other evidence about early humans.

Genetic Testing

Tests now exist for hundreds of diseases that have a genetic component. Many of these are used on fetuses and newborn babies. The most common test for fetuses is called amniocentesis. In amniocentesis, a physician extracts amniotic fluid from the uterus. This fluid, which cushions the fetus, contains fetal cells. The DNA in these cells is analyzed for mutations. If a baby has a severe genetic disorder, some parents may choose to not continue the pregnancy.

Soon after birth, babies have blood drawn to check for a wide variety of genetic diseases. These diseases are mostly ones that are treatable with a special diet or medication. For example, phenylketonuria (PKU) is a disease caused by a mutation in the gene for phenylalanine hydroxylase. This enzyme converts the amino acid phenylalanine into tyrosine, another amino acid. The mutated form of the enzyme is not functional. The buildup of phenylalanine in the bodies of people with PKU causes mental retardation. However, if people with this disorder follow a diet low in phenylalanine, much of the damage can be avoided.

CHAPTER seven

Recombinant DNA

Researchers have developed many different techniques related to DNA. One of the most powerful is recombinant DNA. Recombinant DNA is created by inserting one or more genes from one organism into another organism. This allows the organism with the new gene to make proteins that it normally wouldn't make. Or, the recombinant DNA technique can be used to replace a nonfunctional copy of a gene with a functional one from the same type of organism. Recombinant DNA has a wide variety of uses in agriculture, medicine, and scientific research. However, it also is controversial.

How to Make Recombinant DNA

The process of creating an organism containing recombinant DNA has many steps. For this example, let's say that a scientist wants to insert a human gene into a bacterium. First, proteins called restriction endonucleases snip the human gene out of its normal location on a

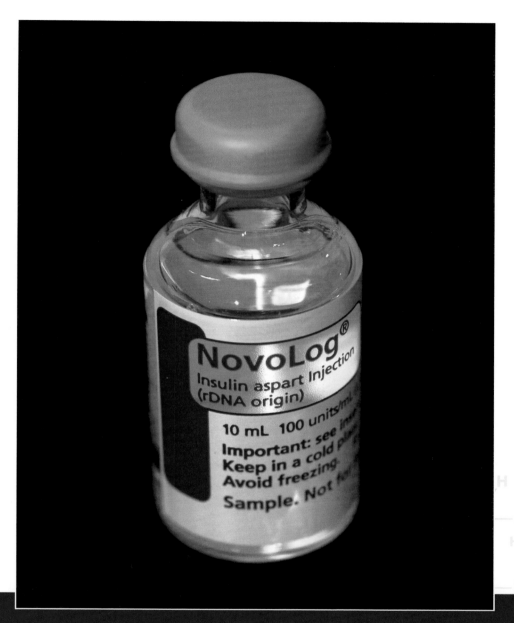

This insulin was produced using recombinant DNA technology. In particular, a human gene was inserted in a bacterium. Insulin was the first of several medically important human proteins to be produced this way.

chromosome. Restriction endonucleases cut DNA only at specific sequences. The scientist needs to know the sequence of the gene and the DNA around it. Then the scientist can choose restriction endonucleases that will cut the DNA before and after the gene, but not in the middle.

The next step is to make lots of copies of the gene. This is done with a technique called the polymerase chain reaction, or PCR. In PCR, the DNA is first heated nearly to boiling. This splits the double helix into two single-stranded pieces. As the mixture cools, primers are added. Primers are short strands of nucleotides that are complementary to short stretches of the gene. The primers bind to the DNA. When the mixture reaches 131 degrees Fahrenheit (55 degrees Celsius), DNA polymerase is added. Most DNA polymerases don't work at this high temperature. The DNA polymerase used is from a bacterium that lives in hot springs. This DNA polymerase attaches nucleotides to the DNA so that it becomes double-stranded again. Then the entire cycle begins again. Using PCR, scientists can make millions of copies of a DNA sequence in just a few hours.

Next, the gene needs to be inserted into the bacterium's DNA. Scientists remove DNA from bacterial cells. The same restriction endonucleases that were used to snip out the human gene are used to open up a hole in the bacterium's DNA. The enzyme DNA ligase is used to connect the human gene with the bacterial DNA.

Then scientists need to insert the recombinant DNA back into a living bacterium. Scientists can perform various procedures to make bacteria more likely to take up DNA from the environment. Researchers have used other methods to insert DNA into other types of cells. Some have employed "gene guns" that actually shoot DNA through cell membranes. Others have loaded the DNA into viruses, which then infect cells. These viruses are altered so that they deliver the DNA, but don't harm the cell. Regardless of how it gets there, after the DNA is in the cell, it should begin making the protein that the gene codes for.

GMO Crops: Revolutionary Discovery or Frankenfood?

Do you want to eat foods that contain foreign DNA? Particularly in Europe, many people have decided that they don't. Genetically modified organisms (GMOs) have been called "frankenfood" in newspapers. People worry that these organisms' long-term safety has not been studied. They also fear that growing GMO crops will have negative effects on the environment. Others claim that GMO foods are completely safe. In fact, some of these crops are more nutritious or require fewer pesticides. Whether or not to eat GMOs is a decision that each person should make for himself or herself after reviewing the available evidence.

Protein-Making Factories

Recombinant DNA has many uses. First, it can be used to make large amounts of proteins. These are usually proteins that are medically or industrially important. For example, recombinant DNA technology is used to make insulin. Insulin is a protein produced by the pancreas that is important for regulating blood sugar. People with some forms of diabetes produce too little or no insulin. Thus, they must regularly inject insulin into their bodies. This insulin used to come from pigs and cows. Insulin from these animals is very similar to human insulin, but some people had allergic reactions to it. After recombinant DNA was invented, researchers inserted the gene for human insulin into a bacterium.

A scientist examines golden rice growing in the Philippines. The plant is genetically modified so that it produces beta-carotene in its rice grains, rather than just in its leaves.

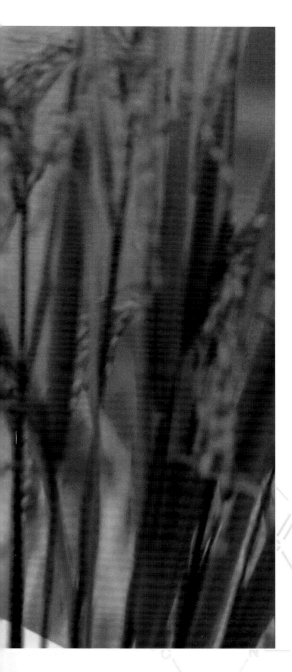

Putting the insulin gene into bacteria was not easy. Human genes contain introns that are later edited out. Bacterial genes do not have introns. Thus, bacteria do not have spliceosomes to edit out introns. Therefore, researchers had to create a copy of the insulin gene that was free of introns to insert into the bacteria.

After they have taken up the recombinant DNA, the bacteria then undergo cell division, creating many tiny factories for producing insulin. The insulin is collected, purified, and shipped to patients. Several other proteins, including human growth hormone, have also been made in large quantities using recombinant DNA.

Genetically Modified Organisms

Organisms that contain recombinant DNA are often called genetically modified organisms (GMOs). These organisms are particularly of use—and concern—in agriculture. For thousands of years, farmers have been breeding plants and animals to obtain desirable characteristics. Recombinant DNA technology allows researchers to insert genes that provide these characteristics.

Golden rice is an example of a GMO. In underdeveloped countries, many children do not get enough vitamin A. Lack of vitamin A can cause blindness. Rice is a staple crop in some of these underdeveloped countries. Rice plants make beta-carotene, a precursor to vitamin A, in their leaves—but not in the grain. Researchers inserted two genes into the rice plant. These two genes allow it to make beta-carotene in the grain. The rice is a golden color instead of white because of the beta-carotene. The human body converts the beta-carotene to vitamin A. The scientists believe that golden rice could help prevent thousands of children from going blind.

A variety of other GMOs exist. Many of these GMOs have extra genes that provide resistance to pests or herbicides. Roundup Ready® crops, for example, are resistant to the herbicide Roundup. Farmers growing Roundup Ready® crops can use Roundup to kill weeds in their fields without worrying that they will kill their crops as well.

Gene Therapy

Gene therapy is a technique that aims to introduce a functional gene into the human body to take the place of a mutated, nonfunctional gene. Gene therapy is difficult because a lot of cells must take up the gene. Bacteria are single-celled organisms. Thus, the new gene only needs to get into one cell. When creating genetically modified crops, the new gene can be put into sperm or egg cells. Then it ends up in all of the cells of the new organism. Putting a gene into a complex organism, like a human, who is already alive and contains millions of cells that need the gene—that's more complicated.

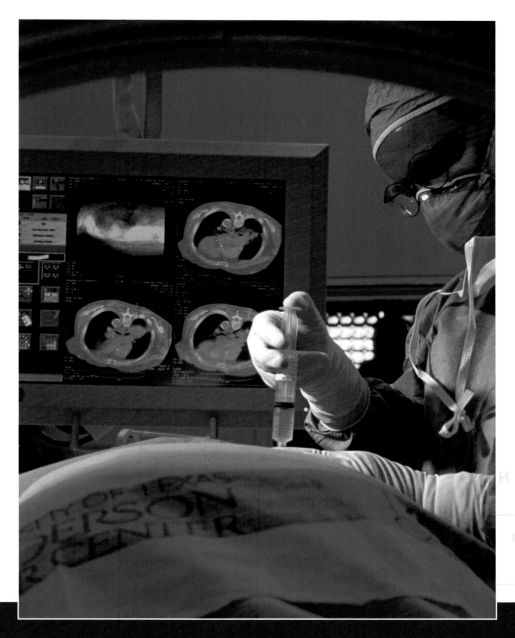

Here, a cancer patient receives gene therapy treatment to his lungs. Gene therapies are still experimental, but they hold great promise for treating diseases of all kinds.

Since many proteins are only important in certain types of cells, the gene may not need to be inserted in every type of cell. But even if gene therapy is limited to one type of cell, that's still a lot of cells.

Most gene therapy uses RNA-based viruses to get genes into cells. Once in a cell, the RNA is reverse transcribed to DNA, which is inserted into a chromosome The RNA-based viruses used in gene therapy are engineered so that they only contain the RNA for the new gene and the components necessary to enter the cell and insert the new DNA into the cell's genome. They are not supposed to be able to cause infection.

Several trials of gene therapy have been conducted. Patients died or became very sick in some of these trials, so they ended early. Many researchers are working hard to develop successful gene therapies. However, it will likely be a long time before gene therapy is a common treatment.

Glossary

amino acid The building block of proteins.

base One of the building blocks of DNA and RNA; can be adenine, thymine, cytosine, guanine, or uracil.

chromosome A long segment of DNA that is specific to a particular type of organism. Humans have forty-six chromosomes.

codon A set of three bases in RNA that specify a particular amino acid.

DNA Deoxyribonucleic acid, the molecule that contains genetic information.

double helix The two-stranded, twisted shape of a DNA molecule.

enzyme A molecule, usually a protein but sometimes RNA, that helps two other molecules react with each other.

gene A stretch of DNA that contains the instructions to make a protein.

genome An organism's full complement of genes.

histones The proteins that protect DNA and help it fold up in the nucleus.

meiosis The process of dividing a cell into four sex cells, each with half an organism's usual amount of DNA.

mitosis The process of dividing a cell into two new cells, each with an organism's usual amount of DNA.

mutation A change in a DNA sequence.

nucleic acid DNA and RNA.

nucleus The location of DNA in eukaryotic cells.

phosphate A component of the backbone of DNA that contains phosphorus and oxygen.

polymerase chain reaction (PCR) A method of obtaining millions of copies of a DNA sequence in a short period of time.

protein Molecules made of amino acids that do the work of a cell.

recombinant DNA DNA that is created by combining DNA from two organisms.

replication The process of creating a copy of all DNA in a cell in preparation for cell division.

ribosome A structure made of protein and RNA where proteins are made in the cell.

RNA Ribonucleic acid, a molecule that is central to the synthesis of proteins.

transcription The process of creating an RNA molecule from a DNA molecule.

translation The process of creating a protein based on the information in an RNA molecule.

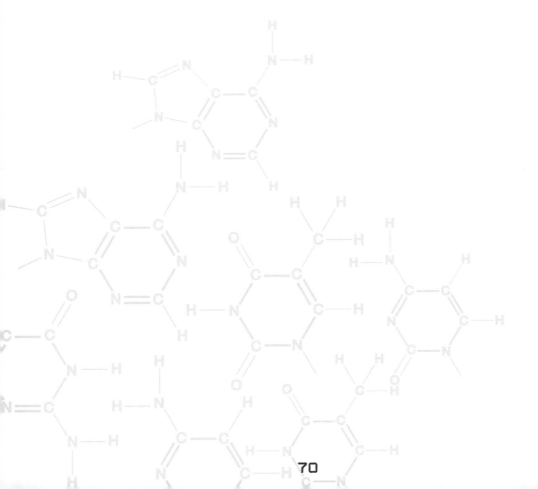

For More Information

American Society for Biochemistry and Molecular Biology
9650 Rockville Pike
Bethesda, MD 20814-3996
(301) 634-7145
Web site: http://www.asbmb.org
This organization publishes scientific journals, advocates for funding for
    research, and supports science education, all with an emphasis on
    biochemistry and molecular biology.

American Society of Gene & Cell Therapy
555 East Wells Street, Suite 1100
Milwaukee, WI 53202
(414) 278-1341
Web site: http://www.asgt.org
This medical and scientific organization helps scientists and the public
    understand genetic and cellular therapies.

American Society of Human Genetics
950 Rockville Pike
Bethesda, MD 20814-3998
(301) 634-7300
Web site: http://www.ashg.org
This organization hosts conferences, advocates for support for genetic
    research, promotes genetic services, and educates the public
    about genetics.

Canadian Association of Genetic Counsellors
P.O. Box 52083
Oakville, ON L6J 7N5

Canada
(905) 847-1363
Web site: http://www.cagc-accg.ca
This organization educates the public about genetic counseling and supports genetic counselors. Genetic counselors help people who are undergoing genetic testing understand their options.

Canadian Society of Biochemistry, Molecular & Cellular Biology
Rob Reedijk
c/o Department of Biochemistry
University of Toronto
Medical Sciences Building
1 King's College Circle
Toronto, ON M5S 1A8
Canada
(416) 978-0774
Web site: http://www.csbmcb.ca
This organization hosts scientific meetings, educates the public, and promotes research in the areas of biochemistry and molecular and cellular biology.

Genetics Society of America
9650 Rockville Pike
Bethesda, MD 20814-3998
(301) 634-7300
Web site: http://www.genetics-gsa.org
This organization brings together geneticists, promotes research in genetics, helps train new geneticists, and educates the public and government about advances in genetics and their potential consequences.

National Society of Genetic Counselors
401 N. Michigan Avenue

Chicago, IL 60611
(312) 321-6834
Web site: http://www.nsgc.org
This organization supports education, research, and public policy
    regarding genetic counseling in the United States.

Web Sites

Due to the changing nature of Internet links, Rosen Publishing has developed
an online list of Web sites related to the subject of this book. This site is
updated regularly. Please use this link to access the list:

http://www.rosenlinks.com/gen/dna

For Further Reading

Canini, Mikko, ed. *The History of Issues—Genetic Engineering*. Farmington Hills, MI: Greenhaven Press, 2005.

Farndon, John. *From DNA to GM Wheat: Discovering Genetic Modification of Food*. Mankato, MN: Heinemann-Raintree, 2007.

Hamilton, Janet. *James Watson: Solving the Mystery of DNA* (Nobel Prize–Winning Scientists). Berkeley Heights, NJ: Enslow Publishers, 2004.

Hunter, William. *DNA Analysis* (Forensics: the Science of Crime-Solving). Broomall, PA: Mason Crest Publishers, 2005.

Innes, Brian. *DNA and Body Evidence* (Forensic Evidence). Armonk, NY: Sharpe Focus, 2009.

Johnson, Rebecca L. *Genetics* (Great Ideas of Science). Minneapolis, MN: Lerner Publications, 2005.

Khumalo, Nonhlanhla P. *Genes for Teens*. Cape Town, South Africa: Yigugu Publishers, 2008.

Levitin, Sonia. *The Goodness Gene*. New York, NY: Dutton Juvenile, 2005.

Lew, Kristi. *Heredity* (Science Foundations). New York, NY: Chelsea House, 2009.

Marx, Christy. *Watson and Crick and DNA* (Primary Sources of Revolutionary Scientific Discoveries and Theories). New York, NY: Rosen Publishing Group, 2005.

Panno, Joseph. *Gene Therapy: Treating Disease by Repairing Genes* (New Biology). New York, NY: Facts on File, 2004.

Polcovar, Jane. *Rosalind Franklin and the Structure of Life* (Profiles in Science). Greensboro, NC: Morgan Reynolds Publishing, 2006.

Schafer, Susan. *DNA and Genes* (Genetics: The Science of Life). Armonk, NY: Sharpe Focus, 2009.

Schultz, Mark, Zander Cannon, and Kevin Cannon. *The Stuff of Life: A Graphic Guide to Genetics and DNA*. New York, NY: Hill and Wang, 2009.

Silverstein, Alvin, Virginia B. Silverstein, and Laura Silverstein Nunn. *DNA* (Science Concepts). New York, NY: Twenty-First Century Books, 2008.

Solway, Andrew. Genetics in Medicine (Cutting Edge Medicine). Milwaukee, WI: World Almanac Library, 2007.

Tagliaferro, Linda. *Genetic Engineering: Modern Progress or Future Peril?* (USA Today's Debate: Voices and Perspectives). New York, NY: Twenty-First Century Books, 2009.

Walker, Richard. *Microscopic Life* (Kingfisher Knowledge). New York, NY: Kingfisher, 2004.

Werlin, Nancy. *Double Helix* (Puffin Sleuth Novels). New York, NY: Puffin, 2005.

Bibliography

Calladine, C. R., and Horace R. Drew. *Understanding DNA: The Molecule and How It Works*. San Diego, CA: Academic Press, 1997.

Carter, Gordon R., and Stephen M. Boyle. *All You Need to Know About DNA, Genes, and Genetic Engineering: A Concise, Comprehensive Outline*. Springfield, IL: Charles C. Thomas Publisher, 1998.

Cowan, Ruth Schwartz. *Heredity and Hope: The Case for Genetic Screening*. Cambridge, MA: Harvard University Press, 2008.

Davies, Kevin. *Cracking the Genome: Inside the Race to Unlock Human DNA*. New York, NY: The Free Press, 2001.

Denis, Carina, and Richard Gallagher, eds. *The Human Genome*. New York, NY: Palgrave, 2001.

Golden Rice Humanitarian Board. "Golden Rice." 2009. Retrieved August 20, 2009 (http://goldenrice.org).

Wade, Nicholas. "Genome of DNA Pioneer is Deciphered." *New York Times*, May 31, 2007.

Watson, James D. *DNA: The Secret of Life*. New York, NY: Alfred A. Knopf, 2003.

Willett, Edward. *Genetics Demystified*. New York, NY: McGraw-Hill, 2006.

Winning, Robert S. "Biol 301—Genetics." Eastern Michigan University. 2006. Retrieved August 20, 2009 (http://www.emunix.emich.edu/~rwinning/genetics).

Index

About the Author

Linley Erin Hall is a science writer and editor in Mountain View, California. She has a B.S. degree in chemistry with an emphasis on biochemistry from Harvey Mudd College and a certificate in science communication from the University of California, Santa Cruz. This is her eighth book for Rosen. She is also the author of *Who's Afraid of Marie Curie? The Challenges Facing Women in Science and Technology.*

Photo Credits

Cover (top) © www.istockphoto.com/Osuleo; cover (bottom), back cover and, interior © www.istockphoto.com/Gregory Spencer; p. 5 © www. istockphoto.com/geopaul; p. 8 © www.istockphoto.com/Andreas Reh; p. 9 © Educational Images, Ltd./Custom Medical Stock Photo; p. 10 CMSP/Getty Images; p. 12 © www.istockphoto.com/Chris Dascher; p. 14 Time & Life Pictures/Getty Images; p. 17 © Lloyd Birmingham/Custom Medical Stock Photo; p. 19 U.S. Department of Energy Genome Programs (http://genomics. energy.gov); pp. 20–21 Peter Lansdorp/Visuals Unlimited, Inc.; pp. 22–23 Robert Holmgren/Peter Arnold, Inc.; pp. 26–27 Omikron/Photo Researchers, Inc.; p. 28 pttmedical/Newscom; pp. 30–31 Popperfoto/Getty Images; p. 35 Image courtesy of the RCSB PDB (www.pdb.org), PDB ID entry 1ehz. The crystal structure of yeast phenylalanine tRNA at 1.93 A resolution: a classic structure revisited., Shi H, Moore PB, RNA, 2000, Aug;6(8):1091–105; p. 36 National Human Genome Research Institute, National Institutes of Health; pp. 38–39 CNRI/Photo Researchers, Inc.; p. 41 SSPL/Getty Images; p. 45 Dr. Gary Gaugler/Visuals Unlimited, Inc.; pp. 46–47 Spike Walker (Microworld Services)/Dorling Kindersley/Getty Images; pp. 48–49 © www.istockphoto.com/ ChristianAnthony; pp. 52–53 Shutterstock.com; p. 54 Stephen Simpson/Taxi/ Getty Images; p. 56 Justin Sullivan/Getty Images; p. 61 Ron Occalea/The Medical File/Peter Arnold, Inc.; pp. 64–65 David Greedy/Getty Images; p. 67 Jim Olive/Peter Arnold, Inc.

Designer: Nicole Russo; Editor: Bethany Bryan;
Photo Researcher: Cindy Reiman

DATE DUE

ARY